FASCINATING WOMEN

by the authors of
A BIBLE STUDY IN MY HOUSE 30-0689-0
JOHN: TOLD WITH LOVE 30-4351-6

FASCINATING WOMEN

A Discussion Guide for Home Bible Study

By

SUE BURNHAM

MOODY PRESS
CHICAGO

ISBN: 0-8024-2530-5

Printed in the United States of America

CONTENTS

INTRODUCTION

Woman's role today is a complex one. Women struggle to balance their time and energy between family, community, and perhaps career.

The question emerges: Is there any pattern which a woman may follow for a lifestyle that will give proper direction and result in fulfillment?

This study focuses on the role of the woman. Questions are designed to help participants find their answers from particular passages of Scripture.

A personal record is included at the back of the book, where goals toward fulfillment may be entered at the conclusion of each chapter.

SUGGESTIONS FOR GROUP BIBLE STUDY

1. Designate one person to be discussion leader. Rotate discussion leaders weekly. Each different personality will make its own unique contribution to the discussion.
2. The discussion leader asks the questions suggested in this guide. After members of the group have made their contributions, the leader can proceed to the next question.
3. Read each section of the Bible aloud before discussing the question. The discussion leader can ask for volunteers to read.
4. You may refer to various translations of the Bible, but do not consult other studies or commentaries during the discussion.

5. Stay on target and avoid tangents. Sharing is important, but long discussions of other subjects can lead away from the main emphasis in a passage.
6. Encourage each member to take part in the discussion. Each member must be concerned and disciplined to listen and participate.
7. Begin and end the study at the agreed time. Allow enough time for the main points in each section and the conclusion.

HER PERSONALITY

Personality is the sum of an individual's characteristics. Each personality is unique, shaped by heredity and various life experiences. Personality is manifested in actions, speech, and emotions.

Jesus Christ imparts a new quality of life to those who believe in Him. This new life is reflected by the personality. Paul revealed a personality which radiated this new quality of life with its stability and joy and peace.

Acts 16 provides historical background for the letter which Paul wrote to the church at Philippi while he was imprisoned in Rome.

READ ACTS 16:12-15

1. What personality traits can be observed in Lydia? How can Lydia be an inspiration for women today?

READ ACTS 16:25-40

2. What heartwarming memories of the Philippians does Paul have to reflect upon while he is in prison writing this letter?

READ PHILIPPIANS 4:1-3

3. What deep emotion does Paul express?

4. What problem does Paul mention concerning two esteemed saints? What tribute does he pay these women? What remedy does he offer?

READ PHILIPPIANS 4:4-7

5. What formula does Paul give for eliminating selfish aims, depression, and anxiety? Describe Paul's own experience (Ac 16:22-25) from which he makes this exhortation.

6. What instruction does Paul give to the dogmatic temperament (v. 5)? What exhortation will stimulate the believer who accepts it to express joy and yieldedness? Why?

7. Which anxieties and perplexing conditions can be relieved by prayer? What is the proper spirit in which to make requests?

8. What is the result of counting on God's wisdom? What keeps the believer's affections pure and his thoughts honest? On what uncertain foundations do some women attempt to build their peace?

READ PHILIPPIANS 4:8-9

9. Name two action verbs which Paul uses in his charge to the believers. How does this charge help you in your daily life?

10. Explain how Christian virtues form the guideline for a woman's life. What will result from practicing these virtues?

READ PHILIPPIANS 4:10-23

11. What conclusion does Paul formulate on the basis of his experiences of suffering? What conclusions about suffering have you drawn? Compare yours to Paul's.

12. What is Paul's attitude toward having abundance? Toward suffering need? What is his source of strength? Of whom is Paul confident?

____

____

SUMMARY

1. Explain how a woman can possess stability (v. 1), tolerance (v. 2), joy (v. 4), and peace (v. 6).

____

2. Describe the six Christian virtues by reading them from various translations.

____

____

APPLICATION

Each day for one week follow the formula of Philippians 4.

1. Thank the Lord for who He is.
2. State your specific needs to God.
3. Think upon the Christian virtues.
4. Now notice and describe the new qualities that God imparts to your personality.

HER POSITION

The issue of woman's position in the world is a complex one. There are a multitude of conflicting opinions and traditions. The Christian woman will want her concepts to be in harmony with God's Word. Genesis 1 and 2 bring the woman's position in the world into perspective, enabling her to evaluate her role in terms of the biblical viewpoint.

READ GENESIS 1:26-28

1. What is the crown of creation (Ps 8:4-7)? In what respect is man unique in all of God's creation?

   ____

2. With what characteristics is the woman created? How, according to the Scripture, do her characteristics differ from the man's?

   ____

3. What privileges and responsibilities does God commission to man? Is woman included on an equal basis? Is this equality practiced today?

   ____

   ____

READ GENESIS 2:7-17

(Genesis 2 gives additional details concerning the events of chapter 1, but it is not arranged chronologically.)

4. From what is man's body fashioned? How is the body transformed into a living being?

____

5. Describe the garden God makes for man in terms of beauty and provision. What specific responsibility does He give to man?

____

6. What opportunity does God provide for man to continue to use his created power of choice?

____

READ GENESIS 2:18-20

7. What does God assert about companionship for the man? What does this imply about the nature of man?

____

____

8. When does the first man become aware that he needs a creation like himself? What intelligence level is indicated?

____

READ GENESIS 2:21-25

9. Of what substance is woman created? What kinship with man is established? Do you think there is any significance in God's creating woman from a rib rather than from another part of the body?

____

____

10. How does the author describe, parenthetically, a priority change in relationships after marriage? What unity is established in marriage?

____

____

11. Describe the attitudes which man and woman held toward themselves and toward each other in the state of perfection.

____

SUMMARY

1. What position in the world did God give woman?

   1:26 ___________________________________

   2:18 ___________________________________

   2:24 ___________________________________

2. Describe the woman.

1:27 ____

2:22-23 ____

3. What responsibilities did God indirectly give her?

1:28 ____

2:15 ____

2:17 ____

APPLICATION

In what additional ways could you subdue the earth in your present circumstances? Ask the Lord to help you fulfill your responsibilities by means of your gifts or talents.

LESSON 3 Luke 1:26-56

HER POTENTIAL

God knew the nobility of character in a peasant woman whom He chose to be the mother of Jesus. Each woman has the potential (latent capability) of serving God fully, but only a few women will obey and sacrifice out of a yielded heart toward Him. Mary had the potential and was willing to live a righteous life and exercise devout faith.

Read Luke 1:1-25 as a background. Other passages concerning Mary include Luke 2, John 2:1-11, John 19:25, and Acts 1:14.

READ LUKE 1:26-38

1. What announcement does the celestial being sent by God bring to the earth? What had been his mission six months earlier (Lk 1:13-19)?

   ____

2. As what does Luke identify Mary? From what distinguished background does Joseph come?

   ____

3. What tribute does Gabriel pay Mary? What position would she have among women? Would this be an honored position today?

   ____

4. How does this peasant girl show that her humility is genuine?

____

5. What great honor does Gabriel describe? How is Mary's virginity confirmed (Mt 1:18)?

____

6. What creative power will bring conception? How is the presence of God symbolized (Ex 40:34)? How does Gabriel describe the child which is to be born from this unique conception?

____

____

7. What tangible fact will validate Gabriel's announcement to Mary?

____

8. What is Mary's response to this announcement of God's will?

____

9. Is her honor as a woman compromised? What sacrifices will obedience entail for her? How does God prove trustworthy (Mt 1:18-24)?

____

____

READ LUKE 1:39-45

10. What trip does Mary eagerly make? State, in your own words, Elizabeth's salutation.

11. For what two reasons does Elizabeth rejoice over Mary? Whose faith is confirmed? Has an understanding friend ever been a comfort to you?

READ LUKE 1:46-56

(Mary's hymn of praise has been called the most magnificent cry of joy ever uttered.)

12. What emotions does Mary express in her hymn of praise? What attributes of God does she name? What additional insights about Mary may be gleaned from the Magnificat?

SUMMARY

1. What do you admire about Mary?

2. What do you admire about Elizabeth?

APPLICATION

You have the potential to be an effective servant for Christ. Ask God to develop qualities in your life (perhaps virtues that you observed in the lives of Mary and Elizabeth) that would please Him. Trust Him for the results.

LESSON 4 | 1 Corinthians 13:1-8a

HER PREFERENCE

When Paul wrote his first letter to Corinth, he included a chapter that has been referred to as the hymn of love. This crowning grace of the Spirit is the most "excellent way" (1 Co 12:31) in all relationships and is especially desirable in marriage.

READ 1 CORINTHIANS 13:1-3

1. Name the various gifts over which love takes preference. How many times is the word "all" used (for emphasis) in comparing the gifts to love?

   ____

2. How can charity be used as a selfish activity? When is martyrdom valueless? What are the motives of women today in using their gifts and giving their possessions?

   ____

READ 1 CORINTHIANS 13:4-8a

3. What two virtues are compatible with love (v. 4)? Which qualities are out of harmony with love?

   ____

4. What happens to love when a misunderstanding arises between a husband and a wife? How does love react when a husband is recognized on account of his success?

5. From what does love separate itself? With what does love choose to identify?

6. When love is present, what kind of manners does a woman display? What temperament can be expected when love is present?

7. What is the attitude of a loving wife toward her husband's motives and mistakes? How does love within the heart of a wife deal with a husband's failure?

8. How is this love, which is God's love, more than a passing emotion? How inclusive is love in relation to people and circumstances?

SUMMARY

1. Describe in your own words the "excellent way" of love which is a necessity in every husband-wife relationship.

APPLICATION

To know how a woman can possess this kind of love, read the following Scripture.

1. Jeremiah 17:9. Describe the condition of the heart without Christ.

   ____

2. Romans 5:8. What provision does God offer for the sinful heart?

   ____

3. 1 John 4:7-10. What is the result of receiving the gift of salvation?

   ____

4. 1 Corinthians 13. Name the specific qualities that God will develop in you as you appropriate His love.

   ____

HER PARTNER

The American woman desires to be attractive to her husband. She attempts to charm him by her outward appearance and clever conversation. Peter, through the power of the Holy Spirit, designs a formula for wives which emphasizes natural beauty, proper conversational techniques, and a gentle spirit. The result is a woman who is fascinating to her husband.

READ 1 PETER 3:1-6

1. What responsibility does a wife have toward her husband? What method may persuade a man to become a Christian?

   ____

2. What do husbands view attentively about their wives?

   ____

3. The following practical suggestions are intended to translate biblical teachings into a guide for daily living.
   a) Develop an attitude of encouraging your husband's leadership.
   b) Thoroughly discuss controversial matters, but let your husband make the final decision. Your experiences, judgment, and viewpoints are vital to the process of reaching a decision, however.
   c) Follow his decision, even though you may disagree with it.

d) A willing spirit in following your husband's leadership brings a release from inner resistance and renewed energy for creative daily living.
e) Trust God for His will to be accomplished through your husband's leadership.
f) Do not follow instructions that break God's laws (Ac 5:29).

4. Explain how a woman's relationship with God relates to her outward appearance. What are your guidelines regarding hairstyle, jewelry, and clothing?
5. What qualities reveal the condition of one's spiritual life? What characteristics distinguished the women of the Old Testament who trusted God?
6. In what particular characteristics should women desire to resemble Sarah? What freedom does this bring?

READ 1 PETER 3:7

7. What attitude is the husband to have toward the wife? In what sense are they strictly equal? In what sense is the wife weaker?

SUMMARY

1. Describe how a wife can be fascinating to her husband based on the formula in this passage.

APPLICATION

1. Compare your attitude toward your husband, in terms of conversational techniques, appearance, and spirit, with the values in this passage. Write down in the spaces of the wheel the areas which need to come under God's control.

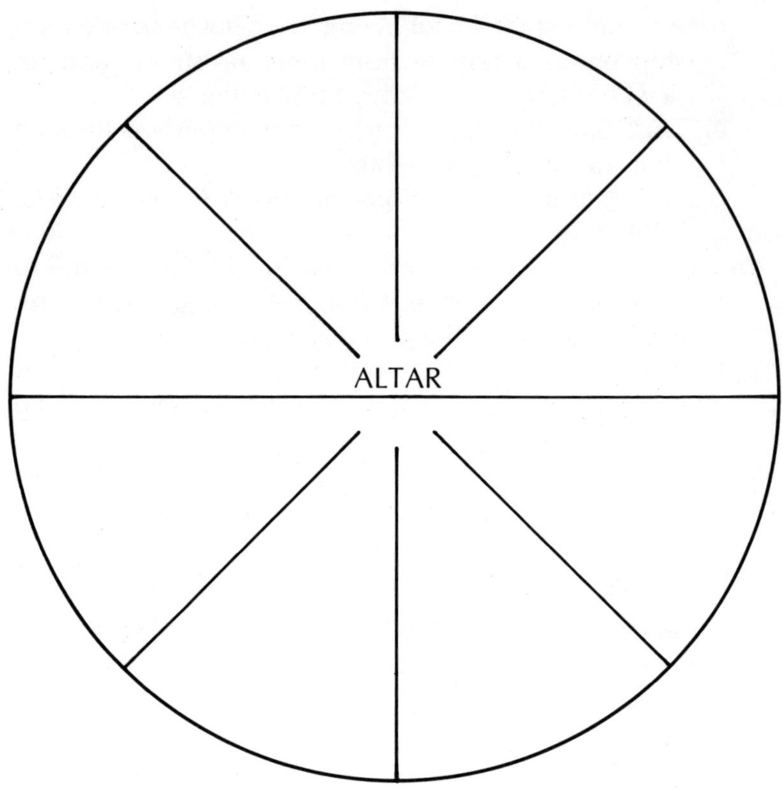

2. Mention in prayer the specific areas which you are willing to place under God's control.
3. Observe His power which will aid you to incorporate these values into your life.
4. Thank Him for fulfilling His promises.

LESSON 6 1 Corinthians 7:1-7

HER PRINCIPLES IN MARRIAGE

Today women may choose among various lifestyles. Some have chosen communal living, in which many partners are available. Some women live on a temporary basis with one partner. Most women live with a permanent partner in the institution of marriage. Paul writes about God's two alternative lifestyles in his letter to the Corinthians. A superstition had crept into the church that marriage was a profane thing. Consequently, an admiration for celibacy had developed. Paul states principles concerning both celibacy and marriage which can be applied today.

READ 1 CORINTHIANS 7:1-2

1. What two lifestyles does Paul present?

 ____

2. What value does Paul place upon celibacy? What advantages does an unmarried woman enjoy (1 Co 7:34)?

 ____

3. For what reason does Paul concede the necessity of marriage? What indirect admonition does he make concerning polygamy?

 ____

READ 1 CORINTHIANS 7:3-5

4. How does Paul counteract the exaggerated spiritualistic tendency which threatened to injure marriage relations? What is the mutual privilege and responsibility of the husband and wife?

____

5. How does Paul's emphasis encourage husbands and wives to steer away from self-love and self-gratification?

____

6. What three conditions warrant interruption of marital relations? Describe situations in which you would have an intense need to free yourself from everything to fast and pray.

____

____

7. What is the danger of continual separation?

____

READ 1 CORINTHIANS 7:6-7

8. What remark indicates that Paul recognizes individual needs? Who can lead a normal life without marriage?

____

9. Is a higher or lower degree of distinction implied (Ro 12:3)? Why do some fail in their celibacy vows?

READ HEBREWS 13:4-5

10. What is God's normal pattern for man-woman relationships? What attitude should govern the marriage bed?

11. What principle should guard our conduct in marriage and in all relationships (Phil 4:11-13)? What comfort to you is God's presence?

SUMMARY

List the principles God has given for marriage in the following passages:

1 Corinthians 7:3

7:4

7:5

Hebrews 13:4 ______________________________

____

13:5 ______________________________

____

APPLICATION

Circle the principles that you need to appropriate in your life. Ask the Lord for His help in fulfilling your privileges and responsibilities as a marriage partner.

LESSON 7 1 Samuel 1—2:10

HER PRAYER LIFE

The fascinating woman receives inner strength from secret, fervent, believing prayer. God honors the prayerful woman today as He honored Hannah over 3,000 years ago.

READ 1 SAMUEL 1:1-9

1. Name the main characters introduced in the first three verses of 1 Samuel.

___

2. What indicates that Elkanah is a wealthy man? Why is Elkanah's homelife disturbed? How does Elkanah attempt publicly to stop the bickering and contention between his wives (v. 5)? What is his attitude toward Hannah (v. 8)? Why doesn't Hannah have any children?

___

___

3. How does Peninnah flaunt her maternity in private and in public? Why do you suspect that Peninnah is jealous of Hannah? Describe cases of jealousy which you have observed.

___

READ 1 SAMUEL 1:10-19

4. Describe Hannah's state of mind. What vow does she make?

5. How does Eli interpret Hannah's sorrowful condition?

6. Why does Hannah's countenance change (in light of the fact that she receives no explicit promise of conception)? Does Hannah's prayer involve more than a petition for conception?

READ 1 SAMUEL 1:20-28

7. In what ways would Samuel's name be important to Samuel, as well as Hannah? What kind of training do you imagine Hannah gave Samuel? (Read 1 Sa 2:26 which suggests the outcome.)

8. Describe the relationship between Elkanah and Hannah (v. 23).

9. How does Hannah fulfill her vow (v. 28)? In what ways can you follow Hannah's example?

READ 1 SAMUEL 2:1-11

10. What does Hannah's prayer express? What indicates that Hannah has triumphed over bitterness?

____

____

11. Whom does she address in verse 3? How is pride in strength and riches discouraged?

____

12. For what other great powers of the Lord does she praise Him? Can any man overcome temptation in his own strength? What future hope does she express?

____

____

SUMMARY

Describe Hannah's deliverance from bitterness and answers to prayer as set forth in the following passages.

1 Samuel 1:10 ________________________________

____

1:11 ____

____

1:15 ____

____

1:16 ____

____

1:18 ____

____

APPLICATION

After you have followed the steps of prayer patterned after Hannah, ask God to fulfill a lack in your life and trust Him for His answer.

LESSON 8 Deuteronomy 6:4-9; Proverbs

HER PRUDENCE AS A MOTHER

Today, many mothers are frustrated in choosing goals and determining how to handle their children. Authorities in the area of child training do not speak with one voice, and consequently many women drift in uncertainty. God's Word presents a curriculum and specific methods by which a prudent woman can train her child. When Moses addressed the Israelites before they entered the promised land, he articulated such a curriculum.

READ DEUTERONOMY 6:4-5

1. What is the foundation of a curriculum for child-rearing? How does this foundation solve the riddle of existence?

---

2. How does the above spiritual principle demand a wholehearted consecration to God? How do you think a loving God prepares a child to love others as himself (Mk 12:28-31)?

---

3. Does your home center around this great commandment?

READ DEUTERONOMY 6:6-9

4. Define "meditating" upon God's commandments. How does that differ from just memorizing them? How does such meditation aid you as a mother?

5. What is the first priority of a parent (Deu 4:15*a*)? Who is responsible for instructing children about spiritual matters?

6. From whom do children receive most of their religious instruction today? How effective are the foster teachers?

7. What two methods should parents utilize in the spiritual instruction of children? How often were the commandments to be taught?

8. What visual aids were to reinforce the teaching of parents? What visual aids can a mother of today use to reinforce her spiritual instruction?

READ PROVERBS 1:7-8

The book of Proverbs, which comes substantially from Solomon, has been called wisdom literature. The proverbs teach practical principles including guidelines for parents and children.

9. Explain how the curriculum of Deuteronomy 6:4 is restated. For what does this proverb teach respect?

___

READ PROVERBS 3:9; 10:5

10. What area of responsible behavior is taught in these passages? Compare it to modern thought on the subject.

___

READ PROVERBS 29:15, 17

11. What methods are an aid in correction? What is the result?

___

12. List qualities, discussed in earlier lessons, that you desire for your child as well as yourself.

   a) Philippians 4 ___

   b) Genesis 2 ___

   c) Luke 1 ___

   d) 1 Peter 3 ___

   e) 1 Corinthians 13 ___

   f) 1 Samuel 1 ___

SUMMARY

1. What is the basic curriculum that Moses presented?

   ____

2. What were the methods of instruction given by Moses and Solomon?

   ____

APPLICATION

Set up a training program for your children for instruction, repetition, and visuals based on Moses' curriculum.

LESSON 9 Proverbs 31:10-31

HER PRIORITIES AND RESPONSIBILITIES

In our society, women struggle to balance wisely their time and energy toward family members, home, community, and perhaps a career. The portrait of the virtuous woman in Proverbs 31 is an ideal from which women may pattern their lives in regard to priorities of responsibilities and character. The influence of a virtuous woman can be a powerful force on society.

READ PROVERBS 31:10

1. For what should a young man search with diligence and discrimination?

____

READ PROVERBS 31:11-12, 23

2. What desirable quality does the virtuous woman possess? In what way is she an asset to her husband? Discuss how a woman can be a hindrance to her husband's advancement.

____

____

3. Explain the difference between genuine love (vv. 11-12) and infatuation.

READ PROVERBS 31:13-15, 27

4. What attitude toward routine work with the hands is implied? What is discouraged?

READ PROVERBS 31:16-19

5. What three activities are mentioned in verse 16? Which one of the three is most difficult for you? What need of the body is preferred above fashion and comfort?

6. What kind of a shopper is this prudent woman? What does the burning candle symbolize?

READ PROVERBS 31:20-22

7. Describe this woman's concern for her family, herself, and others. Which area (family, others, or self) is most neglected in your life?

READ PROVERBS 31:24

8. What financial contribution does she make? Name direct and indirect means by which women can contribute financially to the family.

READ PROVERBS 31:25-26

9. Why does this woman accept the aging process? In what qualities does her beauty reside?

____

READ PROVERBS 31:28-31

10. From whom does she receive blessing and praise? Upon what does her virtue rest?

____

SUMMARY

1. Name her responsibilities and priorities in relationship to others.

   31:11 ____________________________________

   31:15 ____________________________________

   31:20 ____________________________________

2. Name her responsibilities to herself.

   31:17 ____________________________________

   31:22 ____________________________________

3. Name her household responsibilities.

   31:13 ____________________________________

   31:14 ____________________________________

   31:16 ____________________________________

   31:19 ____________________________________

31:20 ______________________________

4. Name her extra contributions.

   31:24 ______________________________

5. Name her character qualities.

   31:11 ______________________________

   31:13 ______________________________

   31:15 ______________________________

   31:16 ______________________________

   31:18 ______________________________

   31:25 ______________________________

   31:26 ______________________________

6. Name the results of following the pattern of the virtuous woman.

   31:28 ______________________________

   31:29 ______________________________

   31:30 ______________________________

APPLICATION

Circle the responsibilities that you need to appropriate in your life. Ask the Lord for His help in fulfilling each area. Trust Him for the results He promised when you follow the pattern of the virtuous woman.

LESSON 10 Luke 10:38-42; John 11:5, 17-32; John 12:1-8

HER PROSPERITY

A woman's prosperity is measured by her values. Some prize money or position; others energy and accomplishment. Jesus told Mary that she had chosen that good part which would not be taken from her. Measured by the value of Jesus, the woman who chooses to know and serve Him has the greatest prosperity.

READ LUKE 10:38-42

Jesus frequently visited friends in the village of Bethany when He traveled between Jerusalem and Galilee.

1. Who extends hospitality to Jesus? What positions do Mary and Martha occupy in the family? Use your imagination and describe this home that Jesus visited.

   ___

2. How does Mary show an interest in her guest? What concern does Martha have for her guest?

   ___

3. What is the cause of Martha's anxiety? How does it affect others? What is the result of your anxiety?

   ___

4. Why does Jesus praise Mary?

READ JOHN 11:5, 17-32

Martha and Mary manifest their faith in varying ways during the events surrounding the death of their brother Lazarus.

5. What confidence does Martha have in Jesus? How is her understanding limited?

6. With what important question does Jesus confront Martha? What does her confession reveal? How would you respond to His question?

7. Compare Mary's and Martha's responses to the presence of Jesus.

READ JOHN 12:1-8

Jesus was strengthened by His personal friends a few days before His crucifixion. Simon the leper honored Jesus with a dinner and the company of friends.

8. Name the principal figures in this story. What is Martha doing? Is this activity consistent with what you already know about her?

9. Why is Lazarus a living witness of the truth? What controversial action is performed by Mary? How does she reveal love, devotion, and humility?

____

____

10. Why is Judas indignant? Is he motivated by love for the poor?

____

11. How is Mary's generosity justified (Mk 14:6-9)? In what way does Mary's gesture help prepare Jesus for the ordeal of the cross?

____

SUMMARY

1. Describe Martha.

   Luke 10:38 ______________________________

   10:40 ______________________________

   John 11:27 ______________________________

   12:2 ______________________________

2. Describe Mary.

   Luke 10:39 ______________________________

   10:42 ______________________________

John 11:32 ____

12:3 ____

APPLICATION

Circle the values that you need to apply in your life. Ask the Lord for His help in knowing and fulfilling His prosperity.

Moody Press, a ministry of the Moody Bible Institute, is designed for education, evangelization and edification. If we may assist you in knowing more about Christ and the Christian life, please write us without obligation to:
Moody Press, c/o MLM, Chicago, Illinois 60610.

YOUR PERSONAL RECORD

Lesson	Long Range Goals	Weekly Goals	Daily Goals
1. Personality			
2. Position			
3. Potential			
4. Preference			
5. Partner			
6. Principles			
7. Prayer life			
8. Prudence			
9. Priorities			
10. Prosperity			